The Incredible Kids' Craft-IT Series

Cut-n-Paste IT

Written and crafted by Pam Thomson
Illustrated by Jeff Shelly

Cut-n-Paste It Contents

Getting Started

Cut-n-Paste It is about more than just scissors and glue. All sorts of wonderful materials can be combined to create lots of exciting projects. In this book, you'll cut and paste many different materials—from magazine clippings to crayon shavings—to create cool crafts and inspire your own original designs.

Go over the "Get It" list with a grownup before you start your Cut-n-Paste It craft so you can get some help gathering your materials. (Sometimes you might need an adult's help with a project, just to be safe.) In addition to your supplies and your grownup, find some old rags or newspapers to cover your workspace—your parents will appreciate it if you keep things clean!

Some supplies in the "Get It" list can be found around your home (such as scissors and white glue), but everything else is readily available at your local art and craft store. Check out the scrapbooking section for fun stationery, funky scissors, and other useful tools. And if an activity calls for a special pattern, look to the back of this book, where you'll find a tear-out section of all the patterns you'll need. If you want to make a pattern bigger or smaller to customize your project, ask an adult to help you duplicate it on a photocopier.

Once you get started, you'll find that the projects in this book are just the beginning of your crafting adventures. You've got a whole head full of fun and crafty—and sometimes zany—Cut-n-Paste It ideas. Feel free to substitute materials or make changes that suit your personal style. Don't hold back—be as creative and imaginative as you can, and make your projects as unique as you are!

Look for this symbol to let you know when a grownup's help is needed.

 Watch It!
Look for this symbol to let you know when special care or precautions are needed.

Seaside Sun Catchers

These melted crayon creatures swirl in the sun to create kaleidoscopic colors!

Don't feel fishy? Draw and cut out your own shapes that reflect your personal style!

Get It!

Sun catcher patterns (page 33)
Wax crayons (wrappers removed)
Pencil sharpener
Wax paper
2 sheets brown craft paper
Iron
Thread or string (optional)
Hole punch
Scissors
Pencil

Tear off around 18" (45 cm) of wax paper, and fold it in half. Place the folded wax paper over a sheet of craft paper on your ironing board, and unfold the wax paper. Set the iron to a medium temperature. (Don't forget to ask a grownup to help you iron safely!)

Gather some different colored crayons, unwrap them, and use the pencil sharpener to make colored shavings. (You'll probably want to use about 12 crayons.) Scatter these evenly, but not thickly, over the bottom half of the wax paper, no closer than 1" (2.5 cm) from the edges. Refold the paper.

Lay a sheet of craft paper over the wax paper, and iron over the paper until the wax melts and blends. (This takes about two passes.) The more spread out the wax is, the more transparent the sun catchers will be.

Let the paper cool; then trace and cut out shapes using the patterns. Punch a hole and attach thread at the top of each shape to hang your sun catchers, or simply tape them in your window. Then let the sun shine in!

Imagine It!

• Instead of hanging your shapes, glue pipe cleaner "stems" to the bottoms of flower-shaped designs to make a colorful bouquet.
• For a creative contrast, decorate the edges of your sun catchers with puffy paint.

⚠ **Watch It!**
Ask a grownup for help when using an iron.

Beautiful Beads

Transform magazines or scrap paper into a wonderful variety of bead necklaces, bracelets, and earrings in minutes!

You can make these beautiful beaded masterpieces when you mix scraps of colorful paper with store-bought beads.

Shell-shaped bead

Bugle-shaped bead

Macaroni-shaped bead

Get It!

Bead patterns (page 35)

Decorative paper (such as stationery, magazine pages, or wrapping paper)

Assorted cordings (like plastic lacing, embroidery thread, or elastic)

Assorted jewelry findings (such as jump rings, clasps, or earring studs)

White glue

Bamboo skewer or knitting needle

Scissors

Pencil

Shell-Shaped Bead

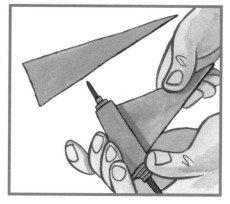

Cut out the pattern from decorative paper. Start at the wide end of the triangle, and roll the paper around the knitting needle, letting it get thicker around the center. When you reach the tip, dab glue on the back, and press it down until dry.

Bugle-Shaped Bead

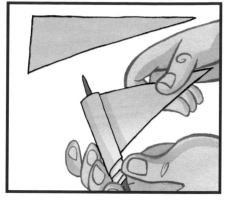

Use the pattern to cut a triangle from decorative paper. Begin rolling around the knitting needle, wide end first. Keep the top edge straight to create the overlapping design. When you reach the tip, glue it down and hold in place until dry.

Macaroni-Shaped Bead

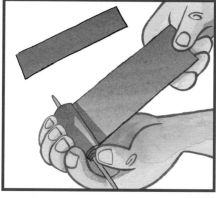

Cut rectangular strips of decorative paper by following the pattern. Start at either end, and keep the edges straight while you roll the strip around the knitting needle. Glue the end of the roll, and press down until dry.

Stringing the Beads

String the beads onto cording to make necklaces and bracelets, or use other jewelry findings for earrings. To create your own unique jewelry, use as many or as few beads as you like. You can even combine different styles or add extra beads.

Imagine It!

You won't have to worry about drying time if you use adhesive-backed paper (such as contact paper) instead of paper and glue. Be sure to leave $1/4$" (6 mm) of backing at the starting edge of the triangle to keep the paper from sticking to the tool.

Magnetic Memos

Scrap paper never looked so stylish as with these "attractive" magnetic notepads!

These adorable notepads make great gifts—and they're fun for passing notes back and forth between friends.

Get It!

Beehive pattern (page 37)
Brown corrugated card stock
Lace daisies
2 yellow ¼" (6 mm) pompoms
Yellow pencil
Yellow pencil-head eraser
White pipe cleaner
12-16 sheets plain paper
Magnet
Small brad
Black acrylic craft paint
White craft glue
Small or medium paintbrush
Scissors
Hole punch

Beehive Memo Pad

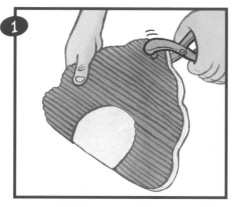

Using the pattern, trace and cut out the beehive shape from both the corrugated stock and the plain paper. Punch a hole at the top of everything, and secure it all together with a brad.

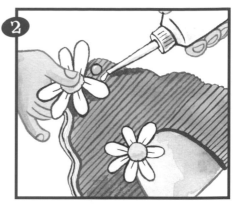

Glue the daisies in place, and then glue the pompoms in the centers of the flowers. (You can substitute the daisies with anything you like, including buttons, fabric patches, or stickers.)

Paint black stripes on the yellow pencil and attach the eraser. Wrap the pipe cleaner under the brad, curling the wire to hold the pencil.

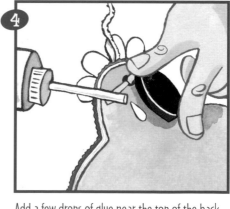

Add a few drops of glue near the top of the back of the notepad. Press the magnet down firmly, and let it dry.

Imagine It!

Make your beehive more original by changing the materials you use. Replace the corrugated card stock with a painted notecard, or use fuzzy pipe-cleaner bees instead of daisies. Whatever you do, make it uniquely your own!

Get It!

Ladybug pattern (page 37)
Red card stock (or substitute thick construction paper)
Green pipe cleaner
Black marker
Red pencil (or a pencil painted red)
Green pencil-head eraser
Googly eyes
12–16 sheets plain paper
Magnet
Small brad
Black acrylic craft paint
Small or medium paintbrush
White craft glue
Scissors
Hole punch

Ladybug Memo Pad

Using the pattern, trace and cut out the ladybug shape from both the card stock and the sheets of plain paper. Punch a hole at the top of all the papers, and secure it all together with a brad.

Using a black marker, draw the ladybug markings onto the card stock. You can make the dots any size you like, and you can add as few or as many as you choose.

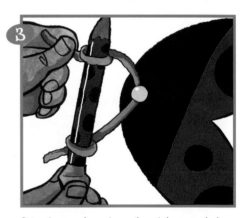

Paint dots on the red pencil, and then attach the eraser head. Wrap the pipe cleaner under the brad, and then curl the wire to hold the pencil.

Attach the googly eyes to the top of the notepad. Then glue the magnet to the back of the notepad near the top, and let it dry.

Get It!

Photo frame pattern with
  tropical flower pattern (page 38)
8½" x 11" (21 x 29.5 cm)
  blue card stock
8½" x 11" (21 x 29.5 cm)
  white label paper or contact paper
Picture or photograph
12–16 sheets plain paper, at least 5" x 5"
  (12.5 x 12.5 cm)
Magnet
Small brad
White craft glue
Scissors
Hole punch
Craft knife
Ruler

⚠️ **Watch It!**
Always ask a grownup for
help when using a craft knife.

Photo Frame Memo Pad

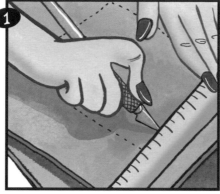

① Have a grownup cut out three 5" x 5" (12.5 cm square) squares from the blue card stock and 12–16 squares from the plain paper. To make the frame, use the pattern as a guide, and have a grownup cut out the center from one blue square with a craft knife.

② Use a pencil to trace the flowered pattern onto the label paper. Then cut out the shapes with scissors. Follow the pattern, and stick the shapes onto the frame. Trim away any excess label paper from the inside of the frame.

③ Glue the picture to the second blue square so it shows through the window on the first. Then glue the first square on top of the second.

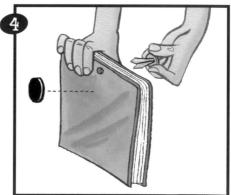

④ Punch holes at the top of all the papers. Secure the frame, paper, and the third blue square with a brad. Glue the magnet to the back.

11

Jazzy Journal

With paper for writing and pockets for pictures, these booklets are perfect memory keepers!

Create a record book that tells about the places you've been and the things you've done—and that shows off your style!

Get It!

Tissue paper in three colors
Assorted colored paper
Two 7$\frac{1}{2}$" x 5$\frac{1}{2}$" (19 x 14 cm) vellum
  envelopes (or substitute white
  envelopes)
6–8 sheets plain paper
Ribbon
Daisy button or other decoration
Plastic wrap
Water-based glue sealer, diluted
  (two parts sealer to one part
  water)
Medium or large paintbrush
Scissors
Ruler
Stapler

1 Open each envelope and trim off $\frac{3}{4}$" (2 cm) below the flap. Fold the envelope in half horizontally. Cut curves across the top as shown. Then set the envelopes aside for use in step 5.

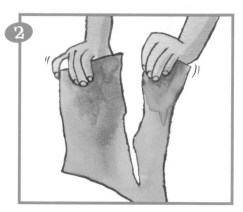

2 Cut the lightest color of tissue into three 9" x 6" (22.5 x 15 cm) rectangles. One of these will become the base for the book. Tear the other colors of tissue paper into long, uneven strips.

3 Place a large piece of plastic wrap on your working surface. Put one rectangle of the light-colored tissue paper on the plastic wrap, and brush the sealer over it. Then lay down the torn strips, one by one. Alternate the color of your strips, and apply the sealer as you layer.

4 Let the laminated paper dry before sealing the last two rectangles of light-colored tissue on the back of the dried piece. Let it dry again, and then trim the cover to 8$\frac{3}{4}$" x 5$\frac{1}{4}$" (22 x 13 cm) before folding it in half horizontally. Round the corners with scissors.

5 Cut the papers to measure 7$\frac{1}{2}$" x 4$\frac{3}{4}$" (19 x 12 cm). Fold them in half horizontally. Alternating with the envelopes, place them all over the cover, and staple them together in the center.

6 Wrap the ribbon around the front cover, and knot it together. Then glue the decoration on top. When it's dry, you can use the ribbon as a place holder inside your journal.

Swirly-Curly Gift Box

When do paper coils rock? When they're rolled into wild-n-crazy circles, ovals, teardrops, and swirls!

The coiling fun doesn't have to stop when your box is done. You also can glue a pushpin or a magnet to the back of the flower heads. Make a whole garden to fill your box!

Get It!

Box pattern (page 39)
Daffodil pattern (page 38)
8½" x 11" (21 x 29.5 cm) sheets of colored
  paper (as shown, one sheet each: lime,
  yellow, orange, purple, and pink)
One sheet 8½" x 11" (21 x 29.5 cm) finely
  corrugated paper
White craft glue
Bamboo skewer or
  knitting needle
Scissors
Pencil
Ruler

How to Roll Coils

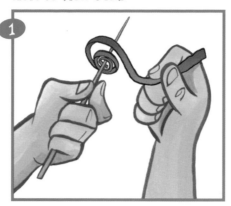

1 Cut at least six ¼" x 8½" (0.5 x 21 cm) strips of each color of paper. Working with one piece at a time, tightly wrap a strip of paper around the bamboo skewer to make a coil.

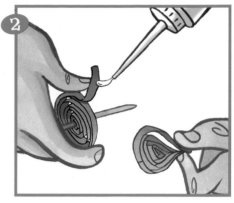

2 Place a dot of glue on the loose end, and gently press it to the coil until dry. Make three coils for the flower centers and four for the leaves. Pinch a leaf coil at one end to make a teardrop shape.

Gift Box

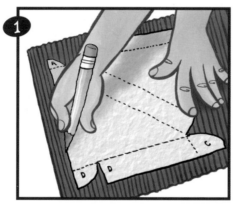

1 Use the pattern to trace the shape of the triangle box on the back of the corrugated stock. Mark the fold lines (the dotted lines on the pattern), and cut out the shape along the solid lines.

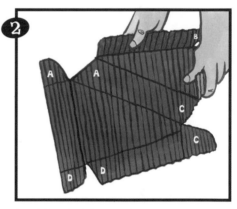

2 Label the tabs A–D, using the pattern for reference. Then fold all the dotted lines inward, toward the center of the box. Crease the lines with a fingernail so they'll hold the shape of the box.

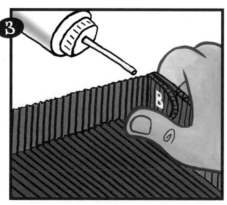

3 Glue each tab to its partner. Put the glue on the back of the small tabs so that they end up on the inside of the box. Let them dry.

4 Use the daffodil pattern to make three flowers from the colored paper. Glue the dry coils to the flower centers, and glue the flowers to the box lid.

Mark-the-Spot Bookmarks

You'll never want to turn the page again, once you've created your own super-cool collage bookmarks!

Flowers and pictures and words—oh my! When you create your own designs, your bookmarks will really stick out!

Get It!

1 roll self-stick laminating sheets
Dried flowers and leaves
White scrap paper
Assorted decorative papers
  and collage materials
  (like wallpaper, memory book
  papers, comics, or catalog and
  magazine clippings)
Assorted ribbon
Small fabric flowers
White craft glue
Scissors
Hole punch
Ruler
Craft knife

⚠ Watch It!

Always ask a grownup for
help when using a craft knife.

Magazine Collage Bookmark

Cut out a 3" x 8" (7.5 x 20 cm) strip of paper.
Then glue on things you've cut out from magazines: patterns, pictures, or whatever you want.

Laminate both sides of the bookmark, and trim
off any excess laminate. Then punch a hole in one
end, and tie a ribbon through the hole.

Die-cut Bookmark

Laminate 3 large dried flowers onto white paper.
Trim a $\frac{1}{4}$" (6 mm) border around the flowers.
Glue the flowers onto a ribbon, 1" (2.5 cm) apart.
Glue the fabric flower to the end of the ribbon.

Hanging Bookmark

Arrange dried flowers on a 3" x 8" (7.5 x 20 cm)
piece of decorative paper, leaving an empty space
between the top flower and the flowers right
below it. (That's where you'll cut a slit in step 3.)

Use a little glue to hold the flowers in place. Then
cover the front and back of the bookmark with
laminating paper, beginning with the front. Cut
around the design, but leave a $\frac{1}{4}$" (6 mm) border.

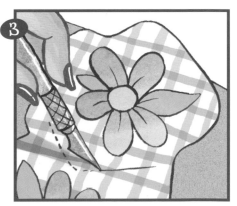

Ask a grownup to use a craft knife to center a
V-shaped cut about $\frac{1}{4}$" (6 mm) below the top
cluster of flowers. Make sure your grownup doesn't
cut all the way across to the sides of the bookmark!

Twinkle, Twinkle Paper Shades

Use different shapes and colors to create your own personal style.

Get It!

- Lampshade pattern (page 35)
- Sheets of translucent paper (such as vellum paper)
- Decorative hole punches
- Decorative scissors
- Large, sharp needle or the tip of a compass
- String of indoor lights
- White craft glue
- Scissors
- Pencil
- Paper clips

Imagine It!
You can add glitter and rhinestones for even more sparkle.

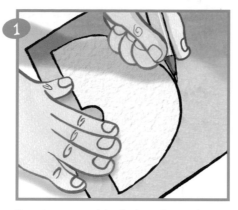

1 Trace the pattern of the shade on the translucent papers, and mark where your hole-punch designs will go.

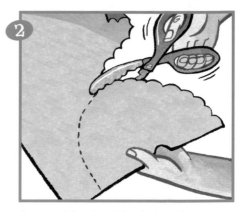

2 Cut around the edge of the shades with decorative scissors, or draw a scalloped edge and cut it out with plain scissors.

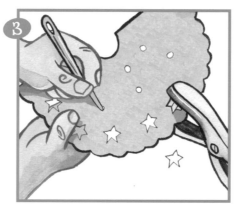

3 Punch holes through the shade from the outside. Use the hole punch for fun shapes along the bottom edge of the shade. Then use the needle to make smaller holes wherever you like.

4 Working with one shade at a time, wrap each shade around a bulb. Overlap the paper to the tab line, and glue it closed. Hold the edges in place with paper clips until they're dry.

⚠ Watch It!
- Always ask a grownup for help when handling sharp objects, like needles.
- Never leave the lights on when you're sleeping or when you're out of the room.

Collage-a-Rama

With the right words and pictures, you can show the world what you think—fashionably!

I WANT TO...

hot

Do You GROOVE

COOL SITES DOT COM

cool

art

Use your charms to create a special bracelet for your BFF—or make one favorite charm into a crazy-cool backpack key chain!

Get It!

Decorative paper
  (such as magazine scraps,
  photos, or scrapbook papers)
6" x 9" (15 x 22.5 cm) piece
  of 6-mm thick craft foam
8" x 12" self-stick laminating
  paper (20 x 30 cm)
Jewelry jump rings
Bracelet or necklace chain
Glue stick
Metal rim tags
Hole punch
Pliers
Water-based glue sealer
Scissors
Small or medium paintbrush
Craft knife

⚠️ **Watch It!**
Always ask a grownup for
help when using a craft knife.

Decorative Charms

Choose some images from magazines or photographs, and cut the images into fun shapes. Then glue them onto the metal rim tags or onto decorative paper backgrounds.

Brush your charms with sealer, and let them dry. This will protect them from being easily damaged.

Punch small holes at the top of each charm. Attach open jump rings to the charms, and loop them through the chain. Ask a grownup to help you use pliers to close the jump rings so the ends meet.

Mousepad

Cut out pictures and words from magazines. Use light dabs of glue to stick the clippings to the foam. Leave at least half of the pad blank so the laminate has something to stick to.

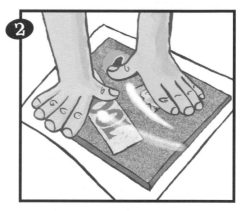

Lay the laminate across the pad. Press down and smooth away all the bubbles.

Turn the pad over, and ask a grownup to trim the excess laminate with a craft knife. If you want, glue cord or ribbon around the pad to give it a little more personality.

Napkin Découpage

When are napkins fun? When they wipe out boredom! Use découpage— a gluing-and-overlapping technique— to liven up ordinary objects.

Follow the flower pot directions to create a funky découpage gift box.

Get It!

Colorful paper napkins
Water-based glue sealer
Flower pot or glass candle holder
    with candle
Scissors
Small or medium paintbrush
Dry cloth

Flower Pot

1 Unfold the napkin and pull apart the layers. Discard any layers without color, and then cut or tear the colorful layers into fun shapes.

2 Brush a small section of the flower pot with sealer. Lay your napkin shapes over the sealer, overlapping the shapes and dabbing on more sealer as you move around the pot.

3 Let the pot dry completely, and then brush a final layer of sealer over the whole pot. Before you use your pot, you'll need to let it dry at least 8 hours (or overnight).

Candle Holder

1 Repeat Flower Pot step 1. Brush sealer on the back of the shapes, and stick each one to the candle holder.

2 Immediately wipe off any excess sealer with a dry cloth (or else it will leave smudges on the glass). Let it dry completely before lighting the candle!

Picture-Perfect Flip Frame

This fantastic frame holds loads of pictures—and shows off your cut-n-pasting talents too!

Your friends and family will think you're the "cat's meow" when you personalize a photo frame with their name and some favorite pictures!

Get It!

8" x 12" (20 x 30 cm) white illustration
    board (or substitute posterboard)
4" x 6" (10 x 15 cm) photo refills
9" x 13" (22.5 x 32.5 cm) decorative paper
1 sheet 4³⁄₄" x 7" (12 x 17.5 cm)
    decorative paper
2 binder rings
White craft glue
Hole punch
Scissors
Craft knife
Pencil
4" (10 cm) ribbon

⚠ Watch It!

Always ask a grownup for
help when using a craft knife.

1 Ask a grownup to use an opened pair of scissors to make a score line in the center of the back of the illustration board, creating two 6" x 8" (15 x 20 cm) panels. Bend the board at the score so the white side is inside the fold.

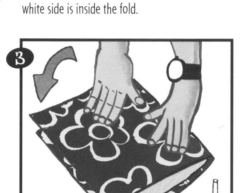

3 Fold the paper over the crease, and glue it to the other panel. Smooth out any air bubbles, and let the glue dry. Ask a grownup to trim off any extra paper with a craft knife. Then glue the ribbon at the bottom of each side of the cover to join the two panels.

5 Hook one binder ring through each hole. Hang the photo refills on one side of the holder, and then turn the binder rings so the hinges are hidden between the two panels.

2 Place the board over the large sheet of decorative paper, leaving ¹⁄₂" (1.5 cm) around all sides. Glue the paper to one panel of the board, and then use your hand to gently smooth out any air bubbles in the paper.

4 Next ask a grownup to use the craft knife to poke two holes through both panels, 2³⁄₈" (6 cm) from the short sides and ¹⁄₂" (1.5 cm) in from the crease. Use a pencil to make the holes large enough for the binder rings.

6 Punch holes in the 4³⁄₄" x 7" (12 x 17.5 cm) paper, ¹⁄₄" (6 mm) from the top and 1⁵⁄₈" (3.5 cm) from the short sides. Loop the binder rings through the cover and close.

3-D Greetings

These funky cards and envelopes are out of this world—you could even say they're from another dimension!

This is a real "window" of opportunity to use your imagination—with cards for any occasion!

Get It!

Window card pattern (page 40)

8½" x 11" (21 x 29.5 cm) colored card stock
(or substitute heavy colored paper)

Decorative paper (such as stationery,
wallpaper, or wrapping paper)

Stickers

White glue

Craft knife

Cutting board (or substitute thick
cardboard)

Standard business envelope

Window Card

1 Fold the long side of the card stock paper accordion style to create a folded card with three separate panels.

2 Trace the window pattern onto a piece of decorative paper. Make sure the paper is a little larger than the folded card panel.

3 Center the decorative paper over the top panel of the card, and glue it in place. (Some extra paper will hang over the panel's edge.) Smooth out any air bubbles with your hand, and then let it dry.

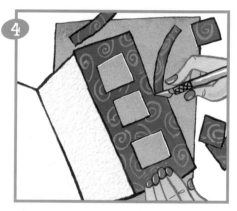

4 Ask a grownup to use a craft knife to cut out the windows through both the paper and the top panel of the card. Then ask a grownup to trim the excess paper off the sides with the craft knife.

5 Place three stickers on the panel behind the cutout windows, being sure to place them so they can be seen through the holes.

6 Glue the top panel to the panel behind it. Press together, and then let the card dry before writing your message inside.

⚠ **Watch It!**
Always ask a grownup for
help when using a craft knife.

27

Get It!

Flower pattern (page 40)

2 pieces 8$\frac{1}{2}$" x 11" (21 x 29.5 cm) colored card stock (or substitute heavy colored paper)

Cotton makeup pads, cotton balls, or toilet paper

4" x 4" (10 cm x 10 cm) scrap of fabric (any color or style)

12" (30 cm) rickrack

Scraps of green paper

Craft knife

White glue

Decorative scissors

Regular scissors

Ruler

Cutting board (or substitute thick cardboard)

Standard gift card envelope

⚠ Watch It!

Always ask a grownup for help when using a craft knife.

Flower Card

1 Cut one piece of card stock to 6$\frac{1}{2}$" x 9" (16.5 x 22.5 cm) and the other to 5" x 7$\frac{1}{2}$" (12.5 x 19 cm). Fold the larger piece in half to create a horizontal card. Then trim $\frac{1}{2}$" (1.5 cm) off the bottom of the top flap with decorative scissors.

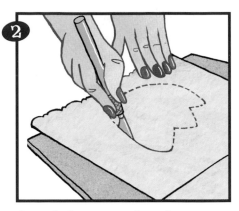

2 Cut out the flower pattern. Center the pattern on the top flap of the card, and use a pencil to trace around it. Ask a grownup to cut out the area within the tracing with a craft knife, creating a flower-shaped window in the top panel of the card.

3 Next use the pattern again to cut out flower shapes from 1–3 cotton pads or several sheets of toilet paper. The more pads or paper you use, the thicker the cushion will be. (You can also use cotton balls for the padding instead.)

4 Place a square of fabric over the window on the back of the front panel of the card, and then glue its edges to the card. The fabric should not be glued too tightly against the card or the padding will not have room to "plump."

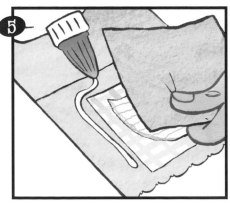

5 Place the padding over the fabric. Glue the second piece of card stock to the flap, over the padding and fabric. When dry, trim away any excess paper.

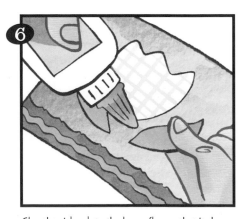

6 Glue the rickrack to the lower flap so that it shows when the card is shut. Glue on leaves cut out from green paper. Let the card dry before writing inside.

28

Get It!

2 pieces 8½" x 11"
(21 x 29.5 cm)
card stock in contrasting colors
(or substitute heavy colored paper)

Confetti

Small balloon

Stickers

3" x 4" (7.5 cm x 10 cm)
plastic sandwich bag

Craft knife

White glue

Scissors

Ruler

Cutting board (or substitute
thick cardboard)

Standard gift card envelope

Confetti Card

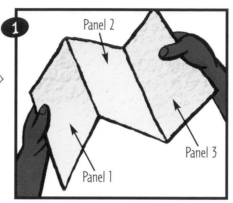

1 Cut one color of card stock to 6½" x 13½" (16.5 x 34 cm) and the other color to 5½" x 7½" (14 x 19 cm). Fold the long side of the larger card accordion style into three panels. Set the smaller panel aside until step 3.

Panel 2
Panel 3
Panel 1

2 Ask a grownup to use a craft knife to cut a 2½" x 3½" (6.5 x 9 cm) window out of the first panel (as shown). Position the window 1¼" (3 cm) down from the top and centered on the sides of the front panel.

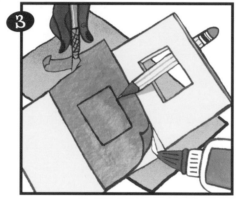

3 Flip the card over, and paste the small panel on top of the second panel, underneath the window of the first. Then trace the rectangle shape of the window onto the paper below. Ask a grownup to use a craft knife to trim away any extra paper beyond the panel's edge.

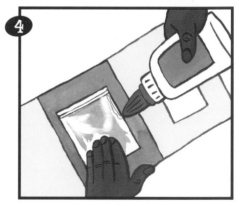

4 Glue around the outline of the rectangle tracing. Then center the plastic bag over the glue (with the opening at top), and press it down along the edges. Check to make sure that the opening at the top of the bag is not glued closed, and then let the glue dry.

5 Press the stickers inside the bag, and arrange the confetti and the balloon. Then glue the top of the bag closed.

6 Glue the top panel to the second panel. Next glue confetti on the front. Let it dry before you write your message inside.

⚠ Watch It!

Always ask a grownup for
help when using a craft knife.

29

Hat-Trick Box

This cool craft will teach you an important lesson: How to keep a secret under your hat!

No one will suspect this ribbon-trimmed hat is actually a box filled with secrets or trinkets!

Get It!

7" (17.5 cm) diameter circle
of cardboard
3³⁄₄" (9.5 cm) diameter
brown craft box with lid
Decorative paper (such as
scrapbook paper, wrapping
paper, or comics)
Assorted ribbons
Jewels, appliqués, and cloth patches
White craft glue
Scissors
Craft knife

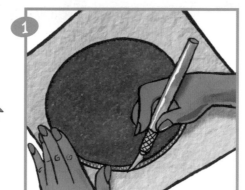

1. Lightly coat the 7" (17.5 cm) circle with glue, and then cover with decorative paper. When dry, ask a grownup to trim away the excess paper with a craft knife. Repeat with a different paper on the other side to finish the brim.

2. Glue the craft box lid to the brim with the top of the lid facing down. Position the lid a little bit off-center, so that it's closer to one side of the brim than the other (as shown). Set the brim aside to dry until step 6.

3. Using the bottom of the box as a guide, trace a circle on the back of a piece of the decorative paper. Cut out the circle, leaving an extra ¹⁄₂" (1.5 cm) of paper around the outside.

4. Every ¹⁄₂" (1.5 cm) around the circle, cut out triangles from the outside of the paper to the inner circle. Glue this circle to the bottom of the box, folding the cut flaps on the sides of the box.

5. Cut a strip of decorative paper ¹⁄₂" (1.5 cm) wider than the box height and long enough to fit around the box. Glue the strip to the sides, over the flaps, and glue the excess to the inside.

6. When dry, set the box into the lid on the brim. Glue a colorful ribbon around the lid and the brim, and place an appliqué where the ribbon overlaps. Then decorate however you like!

Follow-It Project Patterns

This is where you'll find a special tear-out section of all the patterns you'll need. If you want to make a pattern bigger or smaller to customize your project, ask a grownup to help you reduce or enlarge it on a photocopier.

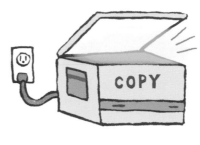

Walter Foster

Walter Foster Publishing, Inc.
23062 La Cadena Drive
Laguna Hills, California 92653
www.walterfoster.com
© 2002 Walter Foster Publishing, Inc.
All rights reserved.

Special thanks to Stephanie Sarracino and the students at Bonita Canyon Elementary School
and to Robyn Allen and the students at Huntington Seacliff Elementary School for their contributions as craft consultants.

Order Code: IT04
ISBN: 1-56010-650-6
UPC: 0-50283-86404-2

Produced by the creative team at Walter Foster Publishing, Inc.:
Sydney Sprague, Associate Publisher
Pauline Foster, Art Director/Designer
Barbara Kimmel, Senior Editor
Samantha Chagollan and Jenna Winterberg, Editors
Carole Thorpe, Production Designer
Toni Gardner, Production Manager
Kathy Beeler, Production Coordinator
Monica Noemi Mijares-DeCuir, Production Artist

Printed in Korea.

Sun Catcher Patterns (pages 4–5)

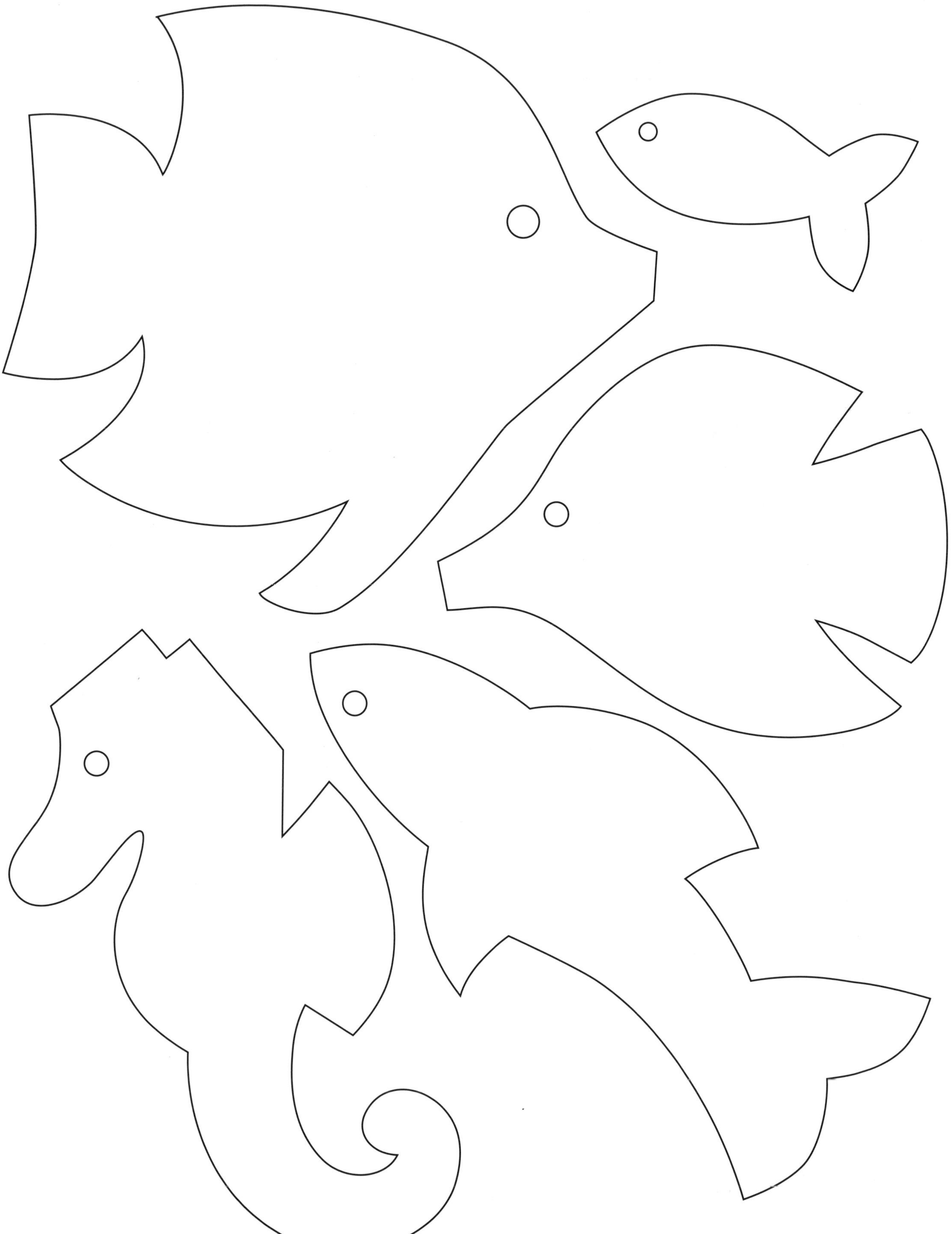

Bead Patterns (pages 6-7)

Lampshade Pattern (pages 18-19)

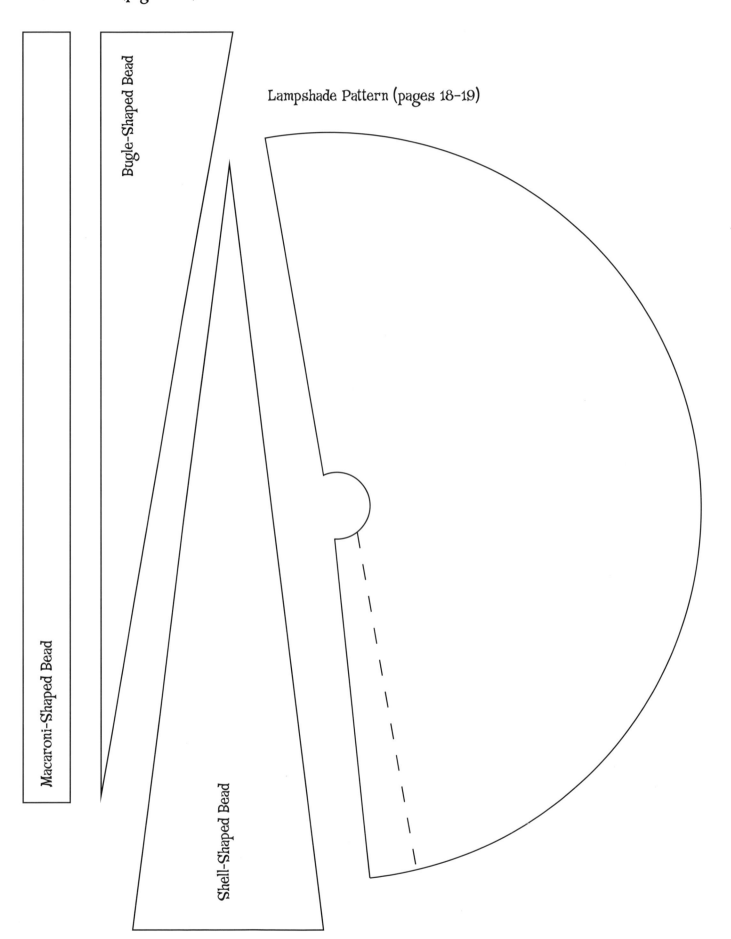

Macaroni-Shaped Bead

Bugle-Shaped Bead

Shell-Shaped Bead

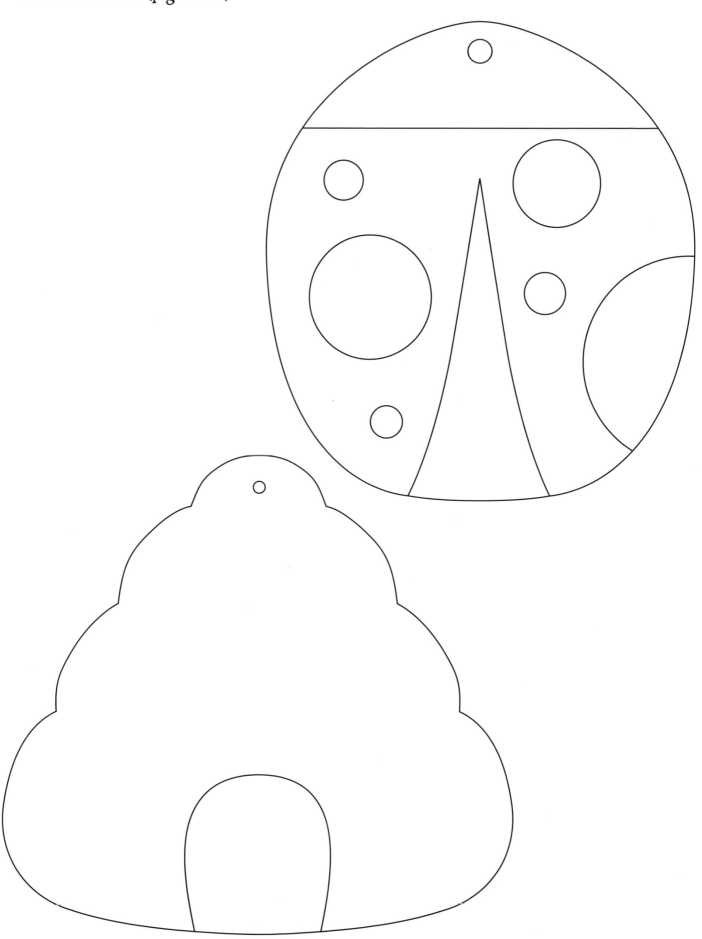

Daffodil Flower Pattern (page 15)

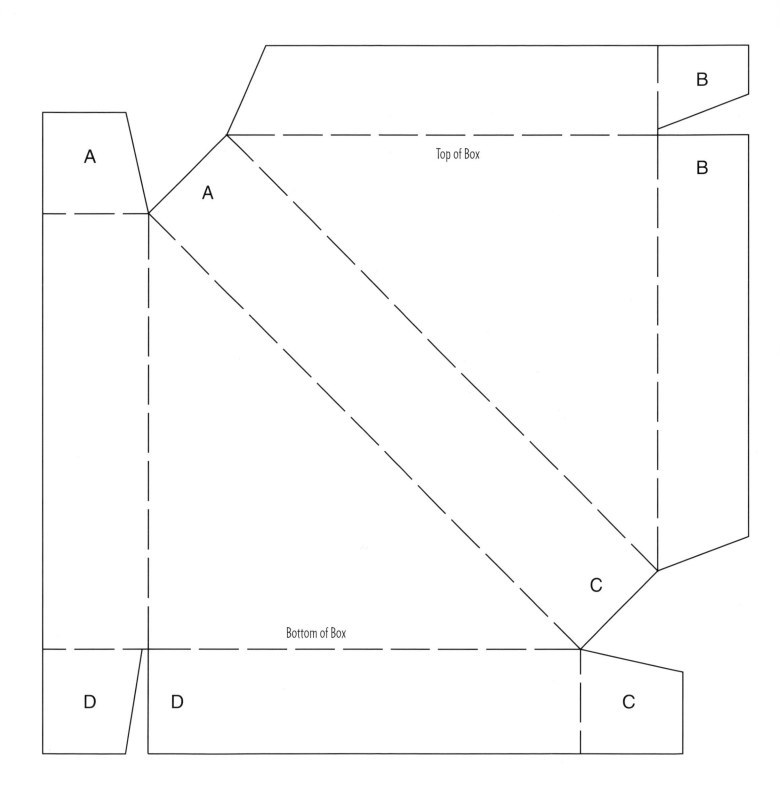

Top of Box

Bottom of Box

Window Card Patterns (pages 26-29)

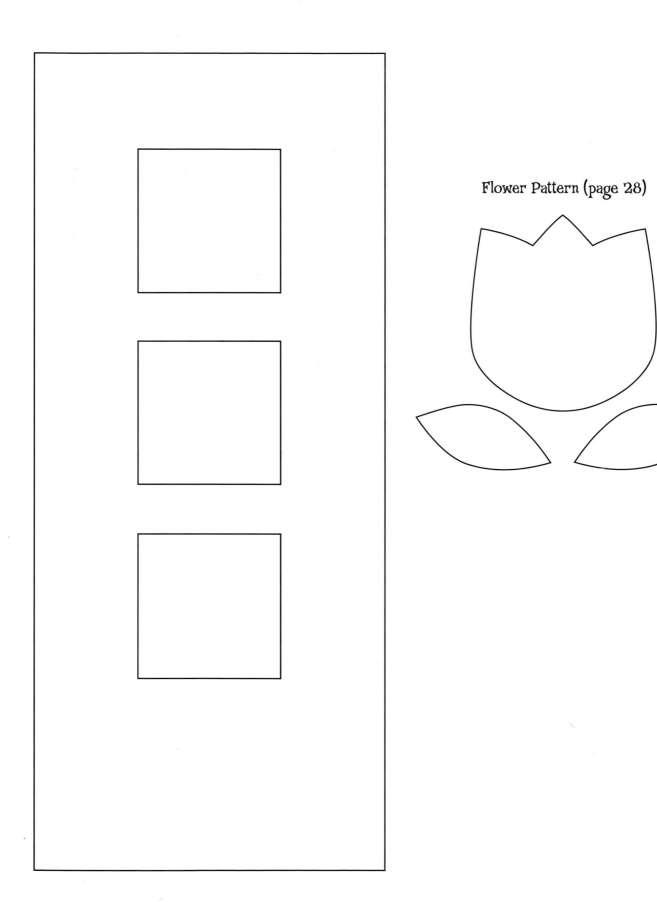

Flower Pattern (page 28)